MW00440479

ASTROLOGY GEMS

CAPRICORN

December 22 – January 19

Monte Farber & Amy Zerner

Sterling Publishing Co., Inc.
New York

Text © 2006 by Monte Farber
Art © 2006 by Amy Zerner

10 9 8 7 6 5 4 3

Published by Sterling Publishing Co., Inc.
387 Park Avenue South, New York, NY 10016

Distributed in Canada by Sterling Publishing
c/o Canadian Manda Group, 165 Dufferin Street
Toronto, Ontario, Canada M6K 3H6

Distributed in the United Kingdom by GMC
Distribution Services
Castle Place, 166 High Street, Lewes, East Sussex,
England BN7 1XU

Distributed in Australia by Capricorn Link (Australia)
Pty. Ltd.
P.O. Box 704, Windsor, NSW 2756, Australia

Printed in China
Sterling ISBN-13: 978-1-4027-4178-4
        ISBN-10: 1-4027-4178-2

For information about custom editions, special sales,
premium and corporate purchases, please contact
Sterling Special Sales Department at 800-805-5489 or
specialsales@sterlingpub.com.

What's Your Sign?

When someone asks you "What's your sign?" you know what that person really means is "What's your astrological sign?" Professional astrologers more often use the phrase "Sun sign," a term reflecting the concept that a person's sign is determined by which of the twelve signs of the zodiac the Sun appeared to be passing through at the moment she was born. The zodiac is the narrow band of sky circling the Earth's equator through which the Sun, the Moon, and the planets appear to move when viewed by us here on Earth.

Astrology's Gift

Astrology, which has been around for thousands of years, is the study of how planetary positions relate to earthly events and people. Its long and rich history has resulted in a wealth of philosophical and psychological wisdom, the basic concepts of which we are going to share with you in the pages of this book. As the Greek philosopher Heracleitus (c. 540–c. 480 BCE) said, "Character is destiny." Who you are—complete with all of your goals, tendencies, habits, virtues, and vices—will

determine how you act and react, thereby creating your life's destiny. Like astrology itself, our Astrology Gems series is designed to help you to better know yourself and those you care about. You will then be better able to use your free will to shape your life to your liking.

Does Astrology Work?

Many people rightly question how astrology can divide humanity into twelve Sun signs and make predictions that can be correct for everyone of the same sign. The simple answer is that it cannot do that—that's newspaper astrology, entertaining but not the real thing. Rather, astrology can help you understand your strengths and weaknesses so that you can better accept yourself as you are and use your strengths to compensate for your weaknesses. Real astrology is designed to help you to become yourself fully.

Remember, virtually all the music in the history of Western music has been composed using variations of the same twelve notes. Similarly, the twelve Sun signs of astrology are basic themes rich with meaning that each of us expresses differently to create and respond to the unique opportunities and challenges of our life.

✦ CAPRICORN ✦

December 22–January 19

Planet
Saturn

Element
Earth

Quality
Cardinal

Day
Saturday

Season
winter

Colors
black, dark brown, gray

Plants
pansy, ivy, tulip, lilac

Perfume
vetiver

Gemstones
jet, obsidian, smoky quartz, turquoise

Metal
lead

Personal qualities
Ambitious, prudent, self-disciplined,
thrifty, and traditional

KEYWORDS

We call the following words "key-words" because they can help you unlock the core meaning of the astrological sign of Capricorn. Each keyword represents issues and ideas that are of supreme importance and prominence in the lives of people born with Capricorn as their Sun sign. You will usually find that every Capricorn embodies at least one of these keywords in the way she makes a living:

status quo • materialism

seriousness and maturity • wisdom

organization • responsibility

structure • crystallization

permanence • tradition • timeline

conservatism • fears • caution

leader of the pack • realism

definition and understanding of

rules and limits • test of time

authority figures • discipline

concern • fulfill obligations • test

concentration • endure restriction

scaling the mountain

leadership potential

Capricorn's Symbolic Meaning

A mountain goat symbolizes Capricorn. The mountain goat is tireless as it makes its way to the tops of mountain after mountain. Most Capricorns are equally tireless in their efforts to get to the top of their respective professions. Most people might think that Capricorns desire above all to attain the respect of the masses. It is more accurate to say that they crave the respect of those whom they, themselves, respect. This is as important to them as is living in wealth and style, yet another way they gain the respect of the "in crowd."

To get to the top, Capricorns are willing to do what is expected of them. This gets them the reputation of being conservative, when deep inside, they are quite sensual. They are conservative in the best sense of the word. Capricorns conserve what they have so that they will have enough when they need it. This is true practicality. Capricorns make wonderful executives. In fact, it is difficult for them to show their true worth until they are left alone to assume some kind of definite responsibility. When they feel this weight resting on their shoulders and realize that the success of the endeavor is up to them, they rise to the occasion, succeeding where others would give up. Once they make something of themselves, they display a kind of energy that can overcome almost any obstacle.

Capricorns display this personality trait because Capricorn is one of the four Cardinal Sun signs in astrology (the other three are Aries, Libra, and Cancer).

Cardinal signs approach life with a great deal of drive. They are enterprising, love to be on the go, and initiate new activities. They accomplish their goals. Capricorn is also one of the three Earth Sun signs in astrology (the other two are Taurus and Virgo). Earth signs respond to the world through their five senses: what they see, hear, taste, touch, and smell. This Earth-element energy gives Capricorns patience, discipline, and a great understanding of how the world works.

Their awareness of how far they have to go to achieve the respect they crave can sometimes make Capricorns pessimistic or, less often, depressed. This tendency actually comes not from the realization of how far they have to go, but from the fact that they rarely allow themselves to become inspired and energized by what they have already accomplished.

Recognizing a Capricorn

A typical Capricorn has a serious look, an "earthy" attractiveness. Capricorns generally do not smile a lot. A Capricorn is quite conscious of appearances, and cares about what other people think. Young Capricorns often look older than their years, and it is also typical for aging Capricorns eventually to become more relaxed and so look younger than their years. They walk with determination and discipline.

Capricorn's Typical Behavior and Personality Traits

* dresses according to convention

* is close to family, even distant relatives

* is somewhat self-conscious

* is quite moody and melancholy

* needs to gain recognition for work

* runs a well-organized home and office

* seems unapproachable

- is dignified and very polite
- appears self-protective
- is cautious when getting to know people
- likes to set long-term goals
- is very reliable
- has strong opinions
- seems as steady as a rock

What Makes a Capricorn Tick?

The lesson for Capricorns centers on the important reason that their life does not provide them with as many opportunities to enjoy success, wealth, and happiness as they would like. They have come into this world with the astrological sign Capricorn because they want to learn the best way to achieve success, wealth, and happiness! They know in their hearts that there are actual techniques they need to learn and lessons they need to apply in their lives before they can attain their full potential.

The Capricorn Personality Expressed Positively

Surefooted and thoroughly practical, in the end the Capricorn goat always reaches the heights, beating others who are faster but less determined. He knows that substance and endurance will win out over flash and style every time. A Capricorn who is true to himself may appear to be somewhat cold and emotionally detached, yet those born under this sign are also generous and kind-hearted.

On a Positive Note

Capricorns displaying the positive characteristics associated with their sign also tend to be:

- good at organizing
- respectful of authority
- cautious, realistic, and conventional
- hardworking and scrupulous
- ambitious and good at business
- people with high standards
- individuals who honor traditions
- givers of sound advice
- calculating before taking action

The Capricorn Personality Expressed Negatively

A Capricorn who is frustrated or unhappy will have trouble getting along with people unless she is the one in authority. Capricorns are emotional but may choose to hide their feelings for fear of appearing weak. They can be a depressing influence on others, due to their rather stoic nature. Because success matters so much to them, they may be opportunistic at times.

Negative Traits

Capricorns displaying the negative characteristics associated with their sign tend to be:

- melancholy
- fatalistic
- rarely satisfied
- cynical and unforgiving
- selfish
- plodding
- manipulative
- egotistical
- loners

Ask a Capricorn If...

Ask a Capricorn if you want a practical solution to a problem. The people born under this sign pride themselves on their common sense. They may not have a glamorous approach to problems, but they know how to get the job done. You can always depend on Capricorns to make an honest and fair assessment. They manage to tell the truth without sounding critical.

Capricorns As Friends

Capricorns are loyal, kind, dependable, and often very generous to friends. They try to prove their sincerity by showing total devotion to the friendship. Capricorns like a friend who is patient, understanding, good mannered, and not too extroverted. They continue to love friends who are old or disabled. They do not desert or neglect loyal friends, no matter how bad the circumstances.

If a friendship fails because of bad judgment on their part, Capricorns can turn very negative. They will brood for days and weeks, mulling over an argument or a poor decision. Capricorns have an irritating habit of recommending things that they think will be good for a friend, but that the friend does not want. At their very worst, Capricorns may ruthlessly use a friend to further an ambition.

Looking for Love

A Capricorn may find that she is attracted to a person who reminds her of the parent she most respected or was disciplined by. This tendency could also manifest as an older person being her perfect partner. Capricorns often seem wise beyond their years, and for this reason they are likely to draw someone older into their sphere.

If a Capricorn does not have a love relationship, the reason is probably related to how she feels about structure, limits, and discipline. A Capricorn may be so disciplined that she does not leave any room in her life for a relationship, possibly because she thinks it will distract her from more serious, important matters. It could also be that a Capricorn does not want to get involved with anyone who displays either too much or too little self-discipline. She must be willing to share the stage with the person she loves and not be adamant about being the one in charge. A Capricorn must be careful not to be too limited in her thinking or unwilling to give people a chance to be human.

If a Capricorn is not in a committed relationship, then one is most likely to come during work hours or through inter-actions with authority figures. It could come at her place of employment, but not necessarily. Partners could tend to be older, and there might be an element of teacher and student in the relationship. Another way this might manifest is if a Capricorn met someone while she was functioning as an authority figure or working on becoming one.

Finding That Special Someone

Because of their devotion to work, Capricorns are likely to find their true love in the workplace or through a professional association of some sort. Since they have a busy social life, they have the chance to meet eligible singles at parties, at cultural events, or through the help of mutual friends. If they choose to use an online dating service, they are likely to keep it a secret from their friends because of their desire for privacy.

First Dates

Try the standard dinner and a movie for a first date for a Capricorn—an old movie, an Oscar winner, would be appropriate. A Capricorn is sure to appreciate it if the evening fits his idea of what a "good date" is. A concert is also a good choice. Capricorns appreciate good taste, so getting together for coffee and dessert at a posh bistro after an event is a good choice. It is always easier for Capricorns to relax and be themselves in an intimate social setting, and a visit to a jazz club or an elegant eatery conforms to their high standards.

Capricorn in Love

Typical Capricorns do not have casual affairs, and they say "I love you" only when they really mean it. They are realistic and down-to-earth and may worry about the emotional aspect of the relationship. Sometimes they must feel financially secure to enjoy love. It might be a good idea for a Capricorn to investigate working with her romantic partner in some practical way. When a Capricorn is in a relationship where she feels secure, then she is caring, considerate, and committed.

Undying Love

Even though Capricorns can fall in love quickly, they don't like to be the one to say the first "I love you." Fears of rejection may cause them to act the part of an aloof lover until the one they have set their eyes on speaks his or her intentions first. Despite this appearance of coyness, once they are part of a couple they are loyal to the point of being dogmatic. Romance often takes them by surprise, allowing them to show a sentimental side. Capricorn doesn't usually make great protestations of love, but will show his love in a hundred ways every day.

Expectations in Love

In their love relationships, Capricorns are very serious. They are usually slow to make approaches and almost never flirt just for fun. Capricorns are not inclined to have casual relationships. They desire to make a home and a family, to make a long-term commitment. Both Capricorn and his partner must state the level of commitment clearly before they make any move toward living together. Living together is the same thing as marriage for some, while for others it is an arrangement of convenience.

A Capricorn expects faithfulness and assumes she will be admired by her loved one. Love and relationships are also wrapped up with her work and career. If a partner is not doing well in those areas, there will be problems in the relationship, since the Capricorn partner may feel the need to criticize or be competitive. Capricorn may fear anyone who might try to impose any kind of discipline, limits, or structure. This would limit the number of people she could have a relationship with, but it is a part of the structure of a Capricorn's being and must be honored.

What Capricorns Look For

Capricorns are sensible people who are unlikely to fall for someone they consider flaky or unpredictable. Their traditionalist views are an important part of who they are, so they usually look for someone who is both serious and stable. They appreciate intelligence, as well as a person who is geared to becoming a success. A nonconformist or layabout is not likely to turn their head, even if good looks are a part of the package.

If Capricorns Only Knew...

If Capricorns only knew how respected and revered they are by the people around them, they would not worry about criticism and gossip affecting their reputation. Capricorns struggle to present themselves honestly, because they are afraid of how others will view them. One reason Capricorns are unwilling to let down their hair is their fear that they will appear to have the normal human frailties. So often they hold themselves to a higher standard, not realizing that it is the quest for perfection, not perfection itself, that makes them admirable.

Marriage

Capricorns seek a partner who has established a good, secure position in life. Rich or poor, if a Capricorn or his partner is not working or enjoying the same level of success or career satisfaction, the relationship will suffer. Capricorn wants a partner who can help him achieve his ambitions. Capricorns tend to be workaholics, and it can be hard to get them home long enough to get relaxed and romantic. They tend to be strong, practical, and successful, however, and can provide their spouses with the best in life. Capricorns are very committed and serious about their lives, homes, and families.

The person who contemplates becoming the marriage partner of a typical Capricorn must realize that Capricorn will take over the organization of the partner's private and professional life. Given this, the person who partners Capricorn can expect responsibility, stability, and security.

Capricorn's Opposite Sign

Cancer is Capricorn's complementary sign, and even though these two are very different, it is possible for stoic Capricorn to learn a lot from Cancer's nurturing ways. Cancers can teach Capricorns how to relax and not take themselves so seriously. Because Cancers are in touch with their feelings, they can also make Capricorns understand that there is nothing wrong with being sensitive. Capricorn's work ethic inspires Cancer to strive harder to achieve goals.

Pairing Up

In general, if people display the characteristics typical of their sign, intimate relationships between a Capricorn and another individual can be described as follows:

Capricorn with Capricorn
Harmonious, but is sometimes a marriage of convenience

Capricorn with Aquarius
Harmonious, although may be somewhat lacking in passion

Capricorn with Pisces
Harmonious, with Pisces nurturing Capricorn's ambitions

Capricorn with Aries
Difficult, yet with plenty of romantic
fireworks

Capricorn with Taurus
Harmonious; a couple who seem to live
in a world of their own

Capricorn with Gemini
Turbulent, with lots of conflicting
ideas and preferences

Capricorn with Cancer
Difficult, yet these two have a lot
to give each other

Capricorn with Leo
Turbulent, but they make a
glamorous pair

Capricorn with Virgo
Harmonious; a true love match if there ever was one

Capricorn with Libra
Difficult, but the challenge is well worth it

Capricorn with Scorpio
Harmonious; an erotically charged relationship

Capricorn with Sagittarius
Harmonious; lovers, friends, and partners in ambition

If Things Don't Work Out

If a relationship begins to fail, it often takes a Capricorn a long time to take action, as she has a strong sense of duty to her partner and her family. In general, Capricorns dislike divorce. Because of their intensely vulnerable nature, they fear the humiliation that comes with a breakup. Also, since the opinion of family members, friends, and even associates means a lot to them, they dislike having to explain a change in their marital or romantic status.

Capricorn at Work

A Capricorn wants to organize the company where she is employed, and she expects absolute loyalty and a disciplined routine. Her job may not be glamorous, but it provides her with a great opportunity to move ahead. Capricorns like coworkers to know that they are punctual and persistent and know how to structure their job and any business systems that they are responsible for in the most efficient and productive manner. By dressing and acting conservatively, Capricorns give a feeling of comfort to those above them.

If mistakes are being made by those in a position to help advance a Capricorn's career, then it is smart for the Capricorn to act cautiously. A Capricorn is calculating and does not want to do anything that might delay her reward or advancement. A Capricorn should do what she can to make things work smoothly, even if she has to fix things in such a way that no one realizes that she is making things work. Capricorn needs to be aware of her tendency to focus on her long-term career goals as much as or even more than on the job at hand. Her competence, professionalism, and perseverance will keep her from failing to do what must be done, but her long-term goals may often be best served by taking care of the day-to-day jobs, especially the ones that others are reluctant to do or unable to do well.

Typical Occupations

The occupations Capricorns usually choose are doctor, dentist, teacher, lawyer, banker, accountant, and any endeavor that deals with prestige or money. They naturally gravitate toward professions or jobs that support the status quo and where they can make a good living for themselves. Their quiet, ambitious natures are perfect for work under pressure. They also can succeed where projects demanding long-term planning are concerned. They generally make good architects, engineers, manufacturers, systems analysts, and researchers. Any occupation that requires good organization and smart management is appropriate for a Capricorn. Many Capricorns are art dealers, jewelers, and managers or agents for entertainers. They also have the ability to turn a failing business around.

Capricorns excel as bureaucrats or politicians due to their skill in debate. Capricorns prefer to work in private. Detail-oriented Capricorns make excellent managers. They are good with their hands, too, and may choose to be in construction or to work with farming, animals, and the land.

Details, Details

No matter how firmly Capricorns have fixed their gaze on the larger picture, they like having a say in the details, too. Capricorns often build their reputation on details, and should look for opportunities to show how worthy of promotion they are. They are sometimes being tested to see whether they should be able to join the club of those who are richer and more powerful than they are. It is important for a Capricorn to show how well she can delegate detail-oriented projects to others, since it can be hard for those born under the sign of the Goat to let other people have a hand in their work.

One of the problems Capricorns have in dealing with details is sometimes making them more important than the entire project. Getting bogged down in small matters can frustrate Capricorns to the point where they can't do their best work. They like having mastery over things, and handling detailed projects gives them this satisfaction. Capricorns need to learn that it is more important to show the full range of their abilities if they want to successfully establish themselves in a way that makes a difference.

Behavior and Abilities at Work

In the workplace, a typical Capricorn:

- must have a comfortable and homey workspace

- is well organized

- is smart with money matters

- plans ahead and makes schedules

- works hard and for long hours

- likes to have food and drink available when working long hours

Capricorn As Employer

A typical Capricorn boss:

- takes responsibilities very seriously

- dresses conservatively and is well organized

- has a strong sense of duty and works very hard

- is kind but expects obedience to the rules

- likes family to visit him at work

- is a good administrator and director of operations

- may neglect personal needs for business

Capricorn As Employee

A typical Capricorn employee:

* stays with a company for a long time

* carries a heavy workload

* is conscientious and dependable

* expects a salary increase with time

* has respect for superiors

* enjoys commonsense assignments

* arrives very early and leaves late

* has an intelligent, wry sense of humor

* minds his own business

Capricorn As Coworker

Capricorns are something of an enigma as coworkers. Whether or not they are in a position of authority, they may instinctively take a leadership role. They are circumspect about their personal life and unlikely to talk to coworkers about life outside the workplace. Once Capricorns start on the road to success, their persistence and ability to focus on a goal enable them to succeed and become authority figures.

Money

A Capricorn should always be conservative in the truest sense of the word, and should get involved in the conservation of resources of all kinds. This includes time, money, possessions, and both natural resources and those that are the result of manufacturing and technological processes.

While Capricorn rules prestige and the status quo, it is more common for people born under this sign to work to achieve a comfortable lifestyle than it is to have been born into money. Capricorns are

materialistic people, though not necessarily in the negative sense of that word.
They don't have to own fine things to
appreciate them and know their worth.
Capricorns are very good at positioning
themselves in situations where they can
accrue a lot of money, and once they
have it, they know how to hold on to it.

At Home

Capricorns take great pride in maintaining a beautiful and well-appointed home. This is a representation not only of their success, but also of their need to create and preserve order in their environment. They are most comfortable in a home that is either like the one they grew up in or like the one they always wanted to have while growing up.

Behavior and Abilities at Home

Capricorn typically:

- likes having a routine
- really enjoys providing for the family
- takes pride in an organized household
- wants quality furniture and fixtures
- needs home as a showcase for business
- is devoted to home and family
- enjoys having visits from relatives
- is skilled as a decorator

Leisure
Interests

Capricorns are so aware of their
duties and responsibilities that they
often find it very difficult to allow
themselves to enjoy anything for its own
sake. Most typical Capricorns are not
much interested in team sports. They
work hard at their hobbies and want to
make a success of them. Whatever
they choose to do, it must be
respectable and increase their
chances of being admired
or honored.

The typical Capricorn enjoys the following pastimes:

* visiting museums and galleries

* golf, walking, playing chess

* gardening and improving the home

* reading best sellers

* music, either listening or playing

* attending exclusive parties

Capricorn Likes

* home and family

* duties and responsibilities

* history, antiques, and genealogy

* the "best" brands

* executive toys

* long naps and pure and simple food

* gemstones and jewelry

* membership at an exclusive club

* personalized gifts and monograms

* new books about old subjects

Capricorn Dislikes

* being pressured
* fads
* surprises
* disrespect
* being teased
* loneliness
* being unprepared
* being embarrassed
* forgetting her to-do list
* cheap quality
* criticism

The Secret Side of Capricorn

Capricorn people have very deep and real emotional needs that can slow them down considerably or even stop them in their tracks. Further contributing to their tendency toward depression are the pressures caused by their desire to maintain a prosperous appearance, keeping pace with both fashion and tradition, while at the same time living in luxury and ease and, in some way, above the level of those whose praises they seek.

Saturn ♄

Saturn is the planet of structure, time, boundaries, restriction, and discipline. It helps people delay pleasure so that they can do what needs to be done in the time allotted. Saturn is a stern teacher, but it can reward individuals for enduring burdens in a mature manner. Conversely, if people shirk their responsibilities, Saturn will show them the error of their ways. Saturn is the last planet usually visible to the naked eye, and so it is associated with going as far as one can go in life, especially in one's career. It also rules automobiles, antiques, and crystals. Saturn is like an anchor, used to prevent people from drifting from where they should be. It rules the bones, teeth, and knees, as well as the sense of hearing.

Bringing Up a Young Capricorn

It is a good to teach Capricorn children the importance of respecting themselves and others for both their inner strength and their outer achievements. Usually, young Capricorns work doggedly at school subjects and aim to get good grades and gain honors. Little Capricorns need plenty of reassurance because they are natural worriers. It is good for them to learn that there is a time and place for everything. One of the unfortunate consequences of the instant TV/movie generation is that they see the story of successful people presented in a couple of hours or less. They have no idea how much dedication, work, rejection, disappointment, and self-motivation are necessary for a human being to build a successful life.

Young Capricorns are not particularly enthusiastic about sports or the out-doors, so they need to be encouraged to spend time outside in the fresh air getting some exercise. Trips to museums, visits to archeological sites, and even rock climbing are likely to satisfy them. They also need to be encouraged to relax and play. They may seem like very serious children, but they have a sense of humor, too. Young Capricorns can have trouble fitting in with other children their age, so they need to be brought into contact with young people who share their temperament.

Capricorn As a Parent

The typical Capricorn parent:

❋ teaches respect and responsibility

❋ takes parenthood seriously

❋ is caring and considerate

❋ will teach children about tradition

❋ is strict with rules but fair as well

❋ has a straight-faced sense of humor

❋ makes sure to provide a good education

The Capricorn Child

The typical Capricorn child:

- is well behaved and responsible

- likes to work on long-term projects

- enjoys setting goals

- can be highly competitive

- worries about her grades

- has respect for other people's things

- is serious but lightens up as he grows older

- usually formulates her life path early on

- has a good though often dark sense of humor

- plays at being an expert or authority figure

- seems older than his years

- likes to stay close to home

- enjoys school and contests of all kinds

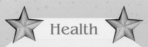

Health

Capricorns need to learn to relax. Worry, long periods of work, and heavy responsibilities could lead to aches and pains and stress-related illnesses. Capricorns need to be careful of depression. They need to make sure to get enough rest at night, and enough light during the day. Capricorns usually exercise only if it fits into their work regime. Knees and bones are likely to

be their vulnerable
body parts. Their resistance
to disease increases with age.
Moderate in their habits, they often
live to a ripe old age.

★ Famous Capricorns ★

Muhammad Ali

Isaac Asimov

Humphrey Bogart

Al Capone

Paul Cezanne

Mel Gibson

Barry Goldwater

Stephen Hawking

Howard Hughes

Joan of Arc

Janis Joplin

Diane Keaton

Martin Luther King, Jr.

Mary Tyler Moore

Kate Moss

Sir Isaac Newton

Richard Nixon

Dolly Parton

Edgar Allan Poe

Elvis Presley

Little Richard

Phil Spector

J.R.R. Tolkien

Denzel Washington

Tiger Woods

About the Authors

Internationally known self-help author Monte Farber's inspiring guidance and empathic insights impact everyone he encounters. Amy Zerner's exquisite one-of-a-kind spiritual couture creations and collaged fabric paintings exude her profound intuition and deep connection with archetypal stories and healing energies. Together, they have built The Enchanted World of Amy Zerner and Monte Farber: books, card decks, and

oracles that have helped millions discover their own spiritual paths.

Their best-selling titles include The Chakra Meditation Kit, The Enchanted Tarot, The Instant Tarot Reader, The Psychic Circle, Karma Cards, The Truth Fairy, The Healing Deck, True Love Tarot, Animal Powers Meditation Kit, The Breathe Easy Deck, The Pathfinder Psychic Talking Board, and Gifts of the Goddess Affirmation Cards.

For further information, please visit: **www.TheEnchantedWorld.com**